FLYING THE RED EYE

Flying the Red Eye

Frank Stewart

FLOATING ISLAND PUBLICATIONS
POINT REYES STATION / CALIFORNIA

ISBN: 0-912449-20-9

Published by:
Floating Island Publications
P.O. Box 516
Point Reyes Station
California 94956

Thanks to the editors of the following magazines, where
some of these poems first appeared:
*Agni Review, Bellingham Review, Cafe Solo, Chiaroscuro,
Floating Island, Graham House Review, Hapa, Hawaii Review,
Indiana Review, Mississippi Review, The Paper, Sonora
Review, Southern Poetry Review, Tendril* and *Tyuonyi.*

"Black Winter" also appeared in *Carrying the Darkness:
American Indochina—The Poetry of the Vietnam War,* Avon,
1985, and in *Peace Is Our Profession,* East River Anthology,
1981. Several other poems were printed in *Reunion,* a chap-
book published by The Paper Press, 1986.

for Pat

Contents

I

II

I

De toda la memoria, sólo vale
el don preclaro de evocar los sueños.

Memory is worthwhile for its one
luminous gift, to bring dreams.

– Machado

Flying the Red Eye

Circling slow and dipping like a fat June bug in the rain,
turbos throbbing in the labored
dark over Chicago, the Electra turned, one wing
pivoted up, like an old dog tilted on three legs,
smelling dank, an old heaviness in him, as though
he were about to tumble over toward those glorious,
snowy lights below. There might have been
freezing sleet as well. In any case, I know
I laughed into a glass half filled with bourbon,
glanced again at the two feathered props
out the window, their cowlings charred and smoky.
But freed all at once from months of killing depression,
elated strangely, almost uplifted.
                                   Below, the groundlights
were steady and beautiful, and nearly everyone else
was asleep, so it was only me
and a couple of pale girls in airline make-up
and the invisible, unspeaking pilots –
                                   and the dark Chicago
lakeside turning slowly underneath. "Christ,
these people will all die in their sleep,"
a voice behind me said to no one.
The bourbon was free as long as we circled,
dumping fuel, swaying and bouncing on the rainy air.
So long a time it almost got dull. The fire trucks
waited below us, grew tired of waiting, no doubt,
their red lights flickering like slow pulsars.

On the wet tarmac in the jeep three hours later,
I almost wanted it all back rather than be down.
And just now the light through a dark window suddenly
and a deep mechanical hum brought it back,
and I wonder how long the circling will last
and whether these small desires since make any difference.

Mount Vernon Parkway

Quick as a tropical lizard, the car rushed over
the humped shoulders of the road, would slant hard,
then pitch back, nipping at the white lines,
at the panicked, oncoming lights. Eighteen
and convertible crazy through a fast autumn.
The colors of the leaves spilled through
the ripped upholstery, the patch-work chassis,
the flaming rust and yellows.
                            In those days
the road forgave everything, and the hours
were long with caffeine frenzy, or blurred
and sweet bourbon crazy.
                            All summer, night
best of all, you sixteen or so. The cold air
whipped our eyes as though it were a sheet,
and the floorboards burned underfoot.

One late August night in the rain
we swerved madly to miss what seemed
some massive helmet
the river had washed onto the road. I stopped,
came back to you with an enormous, snarling terrapin,
threw him onto the floor behind us,
his slimy armor rank and bloody. We turned the car
down into the waves, fought his ripping claws
to haul him out, and plunged him back, against his will
into the putrid tide.
                            He bobbed out like an old shield
and hissed. As if he wanted to be back on land. As if
he wanted the highway, and the black wheels
braking over him.
                            When the weather turned cold,
we'd park late at night, undress, and slip
through the trees along the river's edge,
test the water, our nerves. We'd follow
the maintenance trails, climb the stone walls

and risk a swim in the unlit, heated pools
of the Potomac mansions. The guard dogs barking,
we'd break for the boundary walls, laughing.
The last time, headlong through the woods,
chased by German shepherds that appeared
out of the dark suddenly, I tripped and skidded
face down into the leaves as you ran past,
hard into taut strands of barbed wire. They caught you
below the breast, across the naked waist, and flung you
backward and down, slashed as though with claws, beside me.

We tumbled over the pine fence and lay in the brush
under the low trees. Our game of blood flared
in our adolescent hearts, knowing finally
this was a game of death that we played so hard
because terror was as close to love as we
could get.
               It didn't satisfy us after that.
I disappeared into the South, into war,
then the far Pacific. And you stayed,
acting out the chase
time after time with other men.

It comes back to me here
along the coast called World's End
where the sea bites at the black rocks,
cold and metallic in the tropic winter.
At night I swim here, held in the memory
of your death at the hands of someone
who held you too tightly. I think of your body
by the road near another river, a bite taken
from your brain by gunfire.
               The starlight sags
between the spiked waves, clinging to my arms
and body, like spilled glitter
that I dive to wash away
and dive again and again.

The Firebombing

for L.F. and J.M. and SNCC, 1965

Her easy Jewish smile frail by midnight, Liz
lit the candles – the first cautious light
of our coming home. They illumined the bare
Freedom House walls and the six of us, weary,
glad for shelter, to be indoors and off the Interstate,
a reprieve from the arguing and enlisting,
the constant vigilance.
                  And in that brief, softened
moment, the ceiling like a blow to the face exploded,
the curtained window shattered, the walls fell inward,
and the incinerated air swarmed up,
rat-black with smoke and flame –
the odor of burning hair, gasoline, and mattresses,
the scorched dirt smells harsh as a fist,
like cinched, black rope. And sensation
rang single and shrill. Hammered to fragments.
It went on ringing in the air like an alarm,
and when the falling slowed
a rainy silence settled deep, like the innocent
candles just moments before had been.
                  Those who'd stood
slumped. And those who'd been thrown forward
rose slowly, so for a moment all were hunched
like animals wandering blindly
through an orange haze at dusk. A disembodied
sobbing began, and piece by piece, tending one another,
we walked out onto the street.
                  The white, unmarked cars
circled. Blue lights. And for an instant in the night
everything seemed harmlessly beautiful,
like the slow city's evening traffic

hissing in the rain some quiet freedom hymn
of Jordan just ending.
                              Liz and I drove
place to place that night to comfort
the shattered friends moved to safe beds throughout town,
as if the bomb had blown them all those miles.
But none had died. The logic of that fact
held the world together, for a while, in my young mind.
Liz, I knew, had lived four years with this,
but now she wept and said good night as she let me off.
Jake, her closest friend, had offered
to take me in. "Welcome to Jackson,
white-boy," he said grimly as we reached the door.
And Liz, driving home
                              in the early dawn,
put her car head-on into a tree. Became
that long night's one fatal victim.
Jake on the phone at the morgue was inconsolable.
"Brother," he said.
And though we'd wanted brotherhood, it was not
this kind, which would be lost
over and over. In which we'd be diminished as much
by surviving as by death. This brotherhood
more like hate, like burning, that would leave
none of us wise and young again.

Crossing the Bridge

Mary drives us under the iron needlework
and over the river lights. Dan and I at 4 a.m.
are drunk and feeling so old and ruined
even New York lacks spirit enough tonight
to raise us up. The city sky glows below its smoky tent
toward which we've driven forever, it seems.
The bridge becomes an iron spider's glowing legs
spread over us, stunned and half asleep with long vigilance.

And half sleeping I hear
Dan and Mary's muted voices in front
quarrel, their mutual friends, jealousy,
scores unsettled that I shouldn't hear. My teeth click
with the tires' hum and I sleep.
                                    Dan is crooning
"Brother, Can You Spare a Dime?" thinking of his father
on Riverside Drive, and my own dead father rises
into my dream, and I remember arriving in the dark
like this my first night in New York when he was alive.
Nearly twenty years ago, drunk boy-poet from the South
in the care of Dan, my Broadway friend. Too late
for dinner, he guided me to a dim hotel near a square,
led us through the broken faces and the rotten stairs.

And to a room he'd found for me. We sat on the sagging bed
drinking bourbon from the bottle, talking. Art, poetry,
hope. When he left, the nightmare sleep, the angels
with diesel voices, the ragged lightning
and pursuit came. I suffered, I told him the next day,
friendless in purgatory and the gaping future,
and laughed, "So this is New York."
"Well, I thought you'd want to sleep there," he said,
"that's where Delmore Schwartz died."

Mary turns the radio on and now Dan sleeps,
and I lean over the seat to her. I hate to sleep

in cars, I tell her. I hate radios. I hate New York,
to arrive anywhere at night. I hate the Hudson River
and starlight, traffic, drunks, bad actors,
and all music. Mary smiles back at me in the mirror,
not comprehending, like someone without English
you've asked directions of. "Yes," she says,
"it's good to be home again."

The Bakery

Here is where by four a.m. Rocko
would have mixed already the first
hundred pounder and be pounding the dough
into loaves melon sized, whacking them
like great yellow snowballs, his floury hands
raining the white down in two wide flurries
as he slapped and hammered. And
already he'd be laughing
through a long story on his nephew,
too stupid for school, he'd say, too stupid
even to run numbers, but what a dresser, and
what women that kid brought home. Rocko'd
laugh and pound another loaf as if it were
the nephew's well-tailored shoulder.
And there'd be Mario, listening like it was
a duty to nod and add a word.
By six the pastry bakers had arrived, the
pot washers, shippers, and the place
smelled a way I can't describe, wax and yeast,
sweet grease and laundry, and hot
like the inside of boots. The packers
and drivers came through, shouting,
telling ball scores, optimistic lies
about the lottery, like elixirs for our health –
and delivery men unloading huge sacks
and taking bets, broad-shouldered
men with angelic Italian faces and no English
except "Hey, Rocko" and "So long."
At the bottom of the heap, me and the
pot washers and then Felice – forty-nine, six kids,
no English. Here at lunch he'd teach me
"Parli adagio, per favore," "Mi scusi,"
and "strozzino" and I'd exchange the words
for oranges, muffins, and detergent. We took
common abuse in two languages. I

was young and fought back.
He held on, and here by the ramp
taught me words for snowstorm, the colors,
duty, days and months, and showed me
photographs of Salerno, of small brothers
and sisters and large women smiling. Here
is where I said goodbye to him, secretly
so that no one would hear, leaving a week's pay,
and set out through the snow for California.
It was fifteen years ago, and here is where
I saw him yesterday with Rocko
and Mario and others I didn't know.
More sallow and older. An ordinary day. Nothing
seemed gone between us but accidents and
weather and radio noise. Nothing had come apart
among the proper patterns here, except
there are no more chances in the world.

The Boarder

They opened their doors one by one and came out
into the hall, quietly at first as the morning squeak
of a bare wood floor, the earliest because they thought
they had heard sobbing, or a kind of murmured speech,
like a pulley-rope skidding in its notch.

Which was what it was. And so they found him,
with his back toward them at the hall's end, his hands
dangling loosely like old garden gloves from his sleeves.
His head, which they couldn't see, he'd managed
through the small window of the elevator door –

the glass had been broken out just a day – to watch the car
rise to him from the floor below on its greasy cables and
antique winch.
                    The dark shaft surprised him though. A far
small light instead of darkness, and then the car descended
before he'd time to puzzle out why that filtered light

was where it shouldn't be. It took hours to raise
the elevator car to free him. Workmen climbed the six flights,
stood waiting with heavy saws and useless tools,
and shuffled among the friends half dressed in night
garments, speechless and sobbing, all bewildered,

while other workers sweated at the cables from the roof.
Finally, they carried him down the stairs, covered with red
linen hemmed in white.
                    And why do I not forget him, this stranger,
standing in the quiet, dormitory morning, his head bowed,
staring downward, seeing nothing, as if distracted,

just before the others started wailing? However many years
have passed, we still look up into his face as at a cloud,
or into fate, or at the mild expression on the moon.

Summer 1964 / "O, Freedom over Me"

We waited in the cell, smelling bread
soaked in warm light coffee and the tin
dish they served it in.
                                    And
the smell of jacaranda, green as hay,
and the wind. And a little then of grey walls
and sweating paint, then piss and iron as if
they were the same. Then heard the man's
voice who had beat the two of us,
Jake and me, till the blood lost its taste
and dirt a smell, and fear any definition,
the night before.
                              That morning, all those smells,
the voice hollow in the corridor, and then
the white dust rising on a ladder
of sun against a wall, Greensboro, South Carolina.
Like entering the after-death, as Tibetans
say, severed from the body but thinking still
to have one, light as some silk garment.
But not lightheaded. Jake and me,
burning like silver nails in expectation.

And nothing like it since. Or nearly
nothing – perhaps a certain hour,
an evening with a friend, a cup
of freezing drinking water, the blue on a roof
at dusk, my sister's dead face
beside a South Carolina road.
                                          The cloth
slips on and off, the jailer's hands become
like great bruised flowers he brings us,
Jake and me, singing the only song
we know, infinitely short with infinitely
few words to be so soon over, giving way
to freedom's high butchery.

Black Winter

for a coming time . . .
the boys have memories.

— Jeffers

1

The time between us stretches out
like a winter, lingering farther from the heart,
heavy as fourteen thousand miles of jet and rails.
Looking out, I can't tell whether the glass is crusted
with frost or if I'm seeing the land beyond it,
a white face of resistance. The train from Malmo
thrashes the butcher-cold sleepers, drives me
through the gut of the frozen landscape like a knife.
Deep fog so early. Us. Where can we meet anyone now
except on the edge of ice, anywhere that isn't jungle.

2

They said that Stockholm would turn mortician
slabs of us cold and rootless American boys.
In Montreal the summer before, underground
looking east and north, I met Charles X, he was
with you, "Bright California black boy.
He'll get everything he wants in Sweden." And at first
it was true, you said, in Lund so easy to get dates,
domestic jobs like we all needed. Everything
right. Then the exiles' disease, the common guilts,
assault, journalist's ink. Then lost
the same as if in a jungle, you said. Everyday
the papers full of butchery, "Oriental rubbish
swept into a pile by black & white GIs." But here,
she's sweet, he'd say, she's Swedish pastry, no war,
sweet times. — Someone else's car, six months
into exile, a yellow piece of dress, black billows,
and just small, American, black rubbish on the ice.

3

First night, we sat and watched the Swedish hospital
burn, bullhorn, glare of fire, lights, long engines –
imagining the jungle we'd both escaped beyond Honolulu.
"Exiles should stay out of the sun," you said,
laughing, our lungs cold and tight, so far north
even self-preservation froze. "Along the circle,
the Lapps dance and chant stories through half a year
of night, not for entertainment but to keep
sanity in the darkness. And avoid strong drink."
What of us, survivors here fractured like cold glass,
bits of ghost in ice and heavy smoke. The black
winter is burning out. No one talks of escape.

4

Out by the reef a low fire is burning on the sea,
and in the silent dark a color like old roses
is shining on the swells. When they'd scorch off cover
in those green jungles, the suffocating small hills
would crouch there beyond the flame washed in black scud,
like these waves. Ten years beyond the war now,
on this wharf, I can justify almost nothing so simply
as this fire. The smells of petroleum burning
and brine, carried on the shifting wind, suddenly slam
like a fist that might strike on a cold morning,
unexpectedly, and strikes again, insists and strikes
until there's only blood and burning through the nostrils.
A black mirror. Jeffers: "One should watch and not speak.
And patriotism has run the world through so many
blood-lakes: and we always fall in . . ."

5

On the far horizon the fire is out. The stars
blink on again through the heavy smoke. The Pacific sea
extends again into space. And who did we leave
in the north like ice, and who did we leave there
in the south, scattered on the land like coal?

Travelers

In Stockholm that icy day
the rain blew from the north and then
by noon the sun broke through; by three
the Swedes were outdoors sunning in thin sleeves,
strolling as though it were Easter,
while you and I, like birds of paradise
lost in Lapland, huddled in doorways, bitten through.
Everyone about us smiled at one another; we fought our way
street by street to our hotel, and buried ourselves
under blankets. And sighed at the lonely
displacement. How little we knew then,
newly married, of the cold that finds
the remotest parts of the body to lodge,
that there's no defense except by slow degrees
to become acclimatized. And for a cold this deep
it would take years of freezing.

Why I Love You

That cold last Christmas train rolling
and blowing like an iron boat in heavy swells,
sixty, harrowing the opaque midnight snow,
from Chicago to Lincoln,
from nineteen to the end of your life,
still in your face.

Flight

The choking de Havilland
shakes its wings and dips
at three hundred feet
below the black ceiling,
touches down and taxies easily
toward the old end of the airport.
Seeing Kansas City again, Rose, is not so hard,
though the first time it was
freezing and beautiful – the night, the circumference
burning, illumined still brighter by the cold,
high air and I was waking in your arms
on approach at 2 a.m. half my life ago.
                                      This time
I'm half in love with death, my wife
tells me, fly as though my life were over.
The children have her face, her stunned look,
press around me and wait among the debris
that's mine and not mine. I look out constantly
at the weather, she says, when I should be listening.

Rose, alive then, your hair streaming
against my eyes like power off a black wing tip,
two hundred fifty knots, and a window open,
we lived on air. I know
you were only half in love with me, half
with the speed we kept clear to Kansas City.
Where the world stops overnight, they used to say.
Where some stop forever.
Above all the shitty corn, over the littered towns,
gliding in low tonight alone over the abortions,
the small deaths, the years of waste.
Coming into Kansas City on instruments,
Rose, what a pretty town when you break through.

Don Giovanni

> "I would not have lost so much
> for recreation."
>
> – Jack Gilbert

I have taken everything love's given,
since most were cruel and early on I took
what was brief for the eternal, and the eternal
for the moon, until I too was able
to give back cruelty simply, as a love
who patiently returns a ring, a cache of letters,
a bruise, a half-true story that will alter
the temperature of the night, every night
forever. You will say
I wasted the tide and the ropes
against these wet hulls and every great ship
has left the harbor. You will say I have forgone
the cool center of the lake for blood and rolling foam.
You will say I am an empty pocket.
In answer I might try to give you the long moment
of a young woman who anticipates before a blind,
first date, her pale hands and her ecstasy, wanting
both to lose and remain inside her predictable
days. You have squandered the moon for nothing. –
If I have eaten ashes all my life for love,
still, though old, I found it – cold and unfailing,
a star that circles, looking for the star that's inside
you, no matter how small. Everything else
I have touched steeps and perishes.

Letter to Mary L. (1943–1974)

Overlooking Kahului harbor
a Chopin nocturne plays and your photograph
lies on the table near a book by Gottfried Benn
you gave me – "poet of the morgue,"
your favorite, you said, because
he could forget nothing. The lead-blue water
through the glass, on the horizon. The view
solvent against clutter and the mirror.

In the nocturne there's nothing of Constantia,
of George Sand, her children at Nohant,
hemorrhaging in the lungs, or sanatoriums, the tyranny
of the ordinary – "always in syncopation of feelings
with everyone." The vibration
of the varnished wood, the white porcelain.

Kula Sanatorium glitters like a white nugget
above Makawao, isolated among the trees
on the grey volcanic slope. How many times
I thought of you there, like a cough in a white room,
played the nocturne continually, and fell
into day-long reveries that I drowned
at night in bourbon. The sails
are slowly replaced by running lights, like white
cinders on a black hearth. A star-like flash
comes low over the water on final approach,
then dips out of sight.

Forty

All night the animal sounds
overwhelm. The light is crushed
under the leaves, an odor like failure
and earth. The two sisters.

The wooden boats offshore, the lonely ones
tilted on the sand's highwater mark,
are empty, ears gone deaf, discarded
shells, mud on their skirts.

And the fire has collapsed into the sand.
The mind into the green ditch. A woman I know
is lying next to me, intense with dream
and so far off the light doesn't reach back from her.

I am trying to deserve even the worst
this distance can make occur. Sand
filling the mouths of the roses, something
to fend off the red, nothing but animal sounds.

The tide sends its great arms toward us
like a dumb beast, if only we could fall into them.

Night Music for Insomniacs

for Barbara

How many nights in a lifetime – ?

Hemingway boasted he'd seen
every sunrise.
Us, every midnight.

Sleepless, like oceans,
come to this because of music
and what the ageing
W. C. Fields called his *vision* –

a man in a brilliant white nightgown.

You ask why
write – . Because the unspoiled page
is a sun, the marks that arrive
or don't arrive hardly affect
its eminent brightness.

And it warms us
like phosphorus. Hold such pages
against your heart, consider
the window, the fall –

nothing is worthy of us except music,

and we hear it! We hear it!
although it may be rushing away like
red-shifted stars, or toward us – .
We can't tell.

II

A torch to burn in with pride, a necessary
Ecstasy in the run of the cold substance . . .

     – Jeffers

The Sway Pole Rider

The high circus sounds jangled,
fluted through the colored tents
and up the jeweled shirtfront
of the Milky Way, drawing our gazes out
to the highest stars that shone as though
high on the ear of night.
                          The sky was so tall then
the search beams never came back.
They probed and soared
and disappeared like the light on a miner's hat.
And in the midst of a ring of them
I saw the silver sway pole dancing.
A hundred feet high at least, it bent
like a thin blade of summer grass
in an easy wind that's harmless
but to the frailest things.
                          There was
no wind, though, that night at the Washington
State Fair outside Spokane. Instead, eleven
years old, I saw her – wearing a thin, white,
moth-like cape. By one knee she hung
through a loop, leaned and dipped,
drawing the pole down almost double.
Like a fly rod, I thought, in the slowest
long moment pulled by such deep-running bass
as those in a nearby lake I fished. She
somersaulted slowly over and her red hair, glittering,
spread out wider than that sequined cape,
longer than her long white arms extended.
The sway pole rose, rotating,
bent again. All that I had known of beauty
until that moment evaporated – the dogs, the guns,
girls in magazines, a telescope just bought
and its piercing stars. And then she slipped
her foot into the loop,

launched herself in winding
circles, and I heard the drums, the barker's voice,
the applause inviting her down.
                            I couldn't
get close enough to see her well. Still, I
was surprised she looked so old –
standing on the painted stage above the crowd
of farmers and tradesmen and small children –
to fling her life out, nightly,
that made our breathing stop and the stars
bob behind her like willow whips.
                            When I remember
something good from childhood, I remember her,
even though a week later the radio said the pole
had snapped and she died slowly in an ambulance
as it sped away.
                    No one will come back for the final
week because of that, my father said when he heard it,
standing in the kitchen. "What tempts a person
to do such things," my mother asked.
I listened hard for the answer.
Then we all went on with our lives on earth.

Above June Lake

The seventh day we woke
cold weather had closed down like a grey wing
across the peaks, and only a pinfeather of blue
shone through the gap east toward Mono.
Snow had crusted our gear overnight –
and I rose, light as a bird in the mid-

delirious arms of pneumonia, awoke jubilant
at the gold-grey lake, the thin Sierra air.
The alders and stiff pines, the cliffs and talus
gleamed, it seemed to me, like silver candlesticks.

We'd never camped so high, Russ and me, two young boys –
had toted only spinning reels and light clothes. And
with a ranger's hand-drawn map we'd found the lake,
though a thousand feet higher than it should have been.
Down to nothing now but some canned fruit
and the fish we caught at dawn and dusk.

For me, body had become mind. And the fevered mind
was light and the clear cold things gold light made visible.
Russ grumbled, demanded we descend that afternoon,
for soon I was like the snow itself, unmanageable,
shimmering, ecstatic. We cast our spinners for a last

good meal. In the sizzling pan of mountain trout, we
spooned the last of the canned cherries, made coffee,
then buried what we couldn't carry down. The trek
was long and steep, but Russ insisted we press on –
worried I'd become intractable, though weak, hallucinating
like some Spanish saint free from a lightless prison,
seeing sunlight for the first time, recognizing nothing.

Over the narrow ledge going down through what seemed
like daylight stars I began to fall, and felt the trees brush by
like feathers. I spread my arms, and like a redwing swooped
until the earth was small as a nest toward which I flew.

Overhead, a high flurry that could have been hawks,
some other creature of perfection.
The light closed down fast and I thought
how easy it is to have joy, how easy.

The Pinball Player

for Dean Honma

Right along he might have known
I'd go for the pinball, Four-Stars-A-Thousand,
neon hootchy-kootchy girls poised like Betty Grable
on their toes, back-lit, framed in chrome. Plus
I was only nine or ten, too young to be legal,
and Harry's dispensation to let me play,
risking his tavern license, he said,
made it more forbidden, made my small heart
rush even faster. I stood on a Coca-Cola crate
to play my nickles, slapping at the yellow buttons
that worked the flappers, watching each chrome ball
spin and careen, chiming when it hit a winner,
splashing those smiling neon girls with trembling
baths of colored lights – ping, ping,
ping, chunk, chunk, chunk, ping, ping.
My little hands beat on the yellow buttons
most of a sweltering Georgia morning and afternoon.
                He knew right away I'd play
this forbidden engine and let him just be,
standing with his pals, and then, with him, tell
the women when we got home how we hadn't caught a thing
except mosquito bites, and only stopped for a short one
coming back.
              When we left, the friends laughed
and clapped him on his thin shoulders
and joked about his companion, the pinball player.
In the dusk outside, an odd guilt washed over me.
We rambled home in his truck same as always.
                            It was
years until I hated him properly, the redneck
alcoholic grandfather. Then years more
until I thought continually of him, his one glass eye,
his chain-smoking Lucky Strikes on the sagging porch

and watching the local traffic pass,
talking endlessly of how to bait-fish for bream,
blue gills, and Georgia bass. And years more
until I finally let him be what he required,
what my memory had taken from him, years
to let him go to where it is always
too late to make the good ones rise, to fool women
with thin stories, to talk forever
of what you almost got.

Hard Yellow

"I have faith in liquor and in you,
and both are sweet
like the mystery of church: fall through
and you fall through," my uncle
Bill Bell would say. For years
I forgot him saying it
until once in a hotel room in New York
I woke startled on a mattress
that was smoldering like a loaf of green
bread, the sour smell circling in the air,
and the odor like a bird testing its confinement
in every corner. I could taste the alcoholic future
and heard Bill saying, "Jesus,
the yellow sticks hard."

                  It was the summer
his thin, dapper body had begun swelling
like dough, the smells steeping from him
as his grey mass lay heavy on the floral sheets
under the red-and-green Sears comforter.
The room darkened with death.
                  Day after day
he refused to die, while his poison liver
became the putrid substance of his body.
At first we'd roll him out of bed,
support him, crying
to the formica table for breakfast.
And each day he grew heavier
as though he'd already begun to decay.
It was not easy. I had a new wife then,
and he had an old one, May, who seemed
to tend him well enough while we were there,
but cursed him, too. Cursed us all,
including Arthur, Bill's black running mate
who handled the filthiest part of the work
and ate his lunch out back at May's insistence.

My father told me Bill was Green County's dandy
in his day, drove a Cord and had connections
to the stills, though he drank little then.
His pink skin was always scrubbed clean,
like a baby pig. He bet the dog tracks
in Florida and I remember as a child
his stories of fleet greyhounds and victories
and his lavender smell.
                              But during that last
Georgia August, we all waited and longed
for Bill to let his liver win.
When at last he died, May kicked our asses out,
challenged his will so long in probate
his kin gave up and turned over everything
to her. "I have faith in liquor and in you,"
Bill would tell May in those early, fast days.
I heard him tell it, and then forgot it
and smelled him as he died and coughed
something about yellow sticking hard.
Then I forgot that too. Hard and without mercy,
whatever it was he meant.

Stroke

His maples dropped their leaves
in a bounty there. Unseen birds would make
a rain of motion and shadow, and would light
in tangled boundary wires that held
twisting muscadine and morning glory, so thick
the forest seemed about to burst through
into his yard – heavy with unmown grass and wild
squirrels that chased through the deep, untrimmed lots
on every side. Jack lay four autumn days
in the leaves, until the afternoon I found him
between decay and freezing, and dropped
a blanket about his head and shoulders, as though
for warmth, but more to conceal a final,
deep kiss he and the earth exchanged.

The last of my father's brothers, that year
(a year before my father died at fifty-seven)
Jack refused to say goodbye to anyone –
instead he'd laugh and only turn away
as if his departing guests were simply
stepping out a moment into his yard
to listen to nightingales or smell the jacaranda
and sweet magnolia thick as constellations.
The brothers seemed to have a clock inside them,
set at fifty-six or so, Jack said.
And the best of them go out face down in the leaves
at home, and the worst in a drunk tank
in borrowed shoes. Lucky, he said, the man
who knows the number of his days. Lucky

twice over if it's autumn and the red leaves
and yellow rain haven't given all their kisses away.

Searching for Ice

The quilted snow unrolled and blown overnight
obscures the lake's edge, marked earlier
by the frozen reeds. The frost and wind
break them down, crush their arc into white,
shapeless bristle.
     So five boys with skates
step cautiously out, listening to the crunch
of sole against frozen earth, prodding
with their long sticks, half disarmed
by the serene white, half terrified the ice
will open under them suddenly, then suddenly
shut, washed back, sealing them in blackness,
like a freezer door slamming.
       Just as the skates'
laces cut into their shoulders, their own weight
creases the ice that may be under them. Gravity
seems now to them like a sharp wind to sailors
their senses strain to measure and predict.

As I drive the farm road to work in Barre,
I see them walking there, tenderly, as though
they'd lost a pearl among the morning drifts.
They're weighed down with stories of falling through,
hesitating, just as I am.
      But at dusk, when I return,
they are still there, now princes of snow, regardless
of terrors and cautions, playing in a ring of white.
They'll stay until it's too dark to see the road.
Laughing, they'll go home, having forgotten the early
search, their good luck that the tenuous white
held. Only in stories, they'll think, does it not,
even as the dark is coming down around them
tonight as they skate and sleep.

On the Pali Coast, Hawaii

for Michael Sykes

At dawn the lambs trot the fence perimeter.
At the gate I let them through
and with a dim wedge of silver glass
nailed to the post I shave in the mandarin light
that's slowly igniting the tips of the wild
grass. The wild 'ehako are spinning overhead.
On the dark edge of the grove, the burrowing animals
are still out and busy in the brush.

In that light, feeling more like a lamb than a man,
like moisture on a boot or hat brim, I cross
to the higher fence through the crumbling basalt
and *pili* grass to check the locks
on the high range. I see the rams farther up
posture, halt, and glide away, then strike
defiant poses. The smell of the fresh stems and salt air
burns the chafed skin of my neck and clings
like burrs. The kiawe grove waves its fletchings.

Down the slopes, the deep-running fish
twirl in the green current. The blood in my heart
doubles, flops over and back, startled
at suddenly too much of everything.
Suddenly, something eternal.
"I will touch things, and no more thoughts,"
Jeffers said, in an upcountry like this one,
hearing too the jubilant rhythm
of dancing hooves and wings behind him
and the disobedient wildness.

Christmas Birds

for Shawhan

Through the pastures,
through the rain-soaked rows of chicken pens,
among the squalling cries that crackle
like transformers spattered with rain,
Pascual and I search out two fighters.
          A curious heifer
tries to follow us between the narrow gates,
a grand piano of black muscle that we turn back
with shouts and heavy sticks. Then among his birds
Pascual feeds all but the speckled red
with eyes like Levi buttons, and a white
and iridescent green with beak like a curved awl.

We cradle them gently, carry them down the muddy range
to the house, where Pascual's city friends from Honolulu
are waiting around the Christmas tree.
          In the kitchen
he fastens leather pads, like pale walnuts,
over each bird's severed spur, binding them tight
with rubber bands, and we bring them out
glaring and wild to show. The city friends
have never seen fierce birds so close. Pascual
takes the red, and Larry the other. The men seem
to kiss them, begin to bait them, hold them tightly
and let them stab and wound each other with their beaks.
And then they let them go.
          The birds rush
like tangled feathers and blown weeds in high wind
across the living-room floor, snapping and battering
wings and spiked feet in half flight.

The two men reach in like surgeons and separate them, stroke them
for a moment as if they were tender pets, then
release them again.
                    They rush, spattering together,
their feathers powder away like leaves. Again
and again they're gathered up, and stroked, released
and gathered up. The city friends are unable
to see the rapid hits, to know which has won
and which would be dead.
                        "Here! the red's the winner,"
Pascual shouts, "a champion, a great killer."
"Are they bred to do this?" a friend asks. "They're born
to do it," he says. "This great killer, this great bird."

By the fire that night, the friends retell it
with wonder. In the torn Christmas wrappings
they find red-and-white feathers, some iridescent green,
almost indistinguishable in the colorful paper debris.

The friends drink warm drinks, begin to dance
wildly and happily, stomping the hardwood floors
until the glasses rattle on the black piano,
the pictures tilt on the night walls, portraits
of brothers and sisters not there.
                        And Pascual is dancing
backwards and Larry is leaping until his hair
nearly brushes the ceiling, and the friends at last
are all drunk, some falling, and some going on to the morning.

Letter to a Daughter at Age Ten

The stream has run to jewelweed.
The fallen husks of loquat and rotted plum
increase the litter, the damp smell
of warm decay plays like a mist of insects
steeping over the place
where the stream ends and disappears underground.
I walk there thinking of you,
not watching the way, considering the wildness
in your face as the green forest charge blends
with memory and wish – *We love the things we love*
for what they are, that piece you liked by Frost,
the horror of loss in your small face
I saw night after night and sometimes still –
and reach this place with it.
                              And you
at twenty-five looking back at me, when like my father
I'll be dead early with this disease and will
have given away the paper scratched incessantly
with you in mind. The water of the heart. The dampness.
Inside the leaf of the skin the creatures play,
a certain man wishes and does not wish
that he were part of the massy earth sooner. Sometimes
I think in the stillness more time to think of you
exists, and in pure quiet when the shovels
have quit barking we stop being cruel.
But cruelty is more a part of this than breathing
and keeps on even in things inanimate. I wish
when you're reading this and I'm not there
you'll have forgotten the cruelty done to you.
I could not but wanted to, and was never the same.

Hawaiian Rain

The rain today is a recrimination, a burden,
like dreams, the imagination, overwhelming all
disputes, settling them. Wet straw, duck pond
overflowing, the leaves each suffering it,
like green soldiers in their rain gear, humiliated.

When I think of my father. When I think
of the loneliness here in the mountains that the falling
rain condenses to the size of a face.
When I think of my father's death,
my clothes getting wet, the beds damp, floors
slippery with condensation, the animals standing
stupidly in their pens, the gravel path shining.

It's raining the night my father cried
over the news of his friend's death, when
I was ten, and never again cried in front of me.
When I think of this rain
and how solitary the gravel and trees are
when there is no one here, how solitary
the animals standing stupidly

in their pens when I am away. Rain, like the water
in my body, my mouth, and eyes, and sex. Rain.
And how dry death is, even when it's raining.
How dead they all are, and dry, hearing
nothing underground where all this water seeps.

Moloka'i in a Heartbeat

for Cal

The white egrets fall into the fields, drift
like parachutists, alight
                              as if on springs and follow
the slow cattle that we see from our pickup at fifty –
from Kualapuu, hurling down the green slopes
                                        to the fishponds,

hair flying like spume from sails,
singing, drunk as fish. The mud glitters silver
like blinds on morning windows
between the passing rows of the new green pine,
the wide ravines gape on both sides like great gullets,
choked with kiawe, eucalyptus, enormous trees,
                                        and we
speed on toward a sea on which the whitecaps curl,
go under, then rise like signal flags
in the silent channel – women and men, delirious
on whiskey, wild pig, and friendship. And I wish you
were with us, and the sisters we lost, the fathers
and brothers, old friends gone and dead, as we plummet by
in our speeding truck of endless forgetting.

Weekend

for A. D.

Not young but a beauty still,
she waits on the tarmac for the little
Cherokee of Paradise Air, rests on
her blue overnighter. It's 5:57 a.m.

Scanning the low hills of Moloka'i
in the Pacific quiet, she sits looking inward –
like a fisherman on a tremulous lake
who believes only patience is required
to bring a desire invisibly by.

The sky, grey as powder burn,
lightens to cosmetic silver. And in it
the incoming Cherokee banks,
then touches soundlessly down. Paradise Air

taxies toward her now. The door opens,
the steps are unfolded. She carries her own bags
and meets her pilot just descending –
who retreats for her to enter the wisteria
and silver body, the prop still idling.

A moment later she reappears above the wing
and waves to me in the deserted terminal.
I am not her first love, not mad Willie, not
the Missouri dancer, the saxophonist, the handsome

skier, none of those other weekend friends
she's leaving behind. No, this morning I am only
her driver and wave goodbye. She is so heavy with freedom
how will that little plane ever fly?

The Backwater Poets

for us all

Some look out and see only fire trails disappearing,
ragged forests, broken plains, a watery horizon.
Or flights of lonely mammals, the waterfowl
headed south, arctic plover on the summer trades.
And this Book of Nature almost speaks aloud:
"You're a long ways from New York, aren't you, cowboy?"

Certainly there are no cities to speak of. Forget opera.
The Met, a decent Braque, a single Turner, a Bonnard.
But there are letters. Poems stuffed inside only a dozen others
will ever read, the description of an icy lake,
perhaps, ecstatic winter rain, a sad-eyed waitress
in Upper Michigan a poet could love, heartbreak
and darkness that link us better than print.

Only watercolor: forget ambition. Some lines
like deer holding for a moment in the headlights
before she dives away, a needle in the memory
miles later. And no commerce. No commerce. Just say
an accord, and a certain severity worn lightly.
Names writ in water – and bourbon, and red wine.

Dawn near Polipoli

I look to where the sea tilts
the islands backward over the horizon
where the sea birds are lost as bits of ash
where the atmosphere pales the land and ocean,
then turn again to the table.
Under its glass top the condensing water
nipples and taps to the wooden deck,
a glint of yellow, the wetness having come
from nothing, the colors shimmering from nothing.
A wasp lights stiffly by my arm, flexes
on the damp arm of the metal chair,
drinks and flies on.

A Night Drinking Song

We are driving eighty, neither of us sober,
on autopilot in the fast lane. The chassis lifts
with the wind
         down the long grade from Red Hill
toward Pearl Harbor. The smells
of night sweetness that're like high
spring water wash hard through the open windows
and out again. The lights of the harbor,
like floating gold candles from Delhi,
sputter and flare, marking the black shoreline.
And both of us are singing as though we were new
choir boys,
        as though this tableau were not,
instead, like the quick flash silver bass might show
feeding at dusk, or the hot sweet smell
of a lamp left burning till morning.
          Here
between the old poisons and the surge of new
intention, for an instant between body and memory,
booming through with no gravity in this poor,
fast-flying Datsun.
        I write it down, though already
I lose the faith of it. In its crude roar
and its art, I want to go home and find my lost
brother there, to comfort my few loves
with what little evidence I have, things
burned by the flash into this white wall.

DESIGNED AND PRODUCED BY MICHAEL SYKES AT ARCHETYPE WEST
IN POINT REYES STATION, CALIFORNIA.
PRINTED AND BOUND IN AN EDITION OF ONE THOUSAND COPIES
BY MCNAUGHTON & GUNN, INC., ANN ARBOR, MICHIGAN.
THE TYPE FACE IS KENNERLEY OLD STYLE.

Peter Wild, *Barn Fires*
    32 pp, perfectbound, $3.00
Frank Graziano, *Desemboque*
    48 pp, perfectbound, $4.00
Christine Zawadiwsky, *Sleeping With The Enemy*
    32 pp, perfectbound, $4.00
Jeffery Beam, *The Golden Legend*
    48 pp, perfectbound, $5.00
David Hilton, *Penguins*
    24 pp, hand-sewn, $3.00
Joanne Kyger, *Up My Coast*
    24 pp, hand-sewn, $3.00
Frank Stewart, *The Open Water*
    64 pp, perfectbound, $5.00
Arthur Sze, *Dazzled*
    60 pp, perfectbound, $5.00
John Brandi, *The Cowboy from Phantom Banks*
    80 pp, smythe-sewn, $6.95
Peter Wild, *The Light on Little Mormon Lake*
    32 pp, hand-sewn, $4.00
Kirk Robertson, *Two Weeks Off*
    48 pp, hand-sewn, $5.00
Norbert Krapf, *Circus Songs*
    32 pp, hand-sewn, $4.00
Cole Swensen, *It's Alive She Says*
    88 pp, smythe-sewn, $5.00
Joan Wolf, *The Divided Sphere*
    96 pp, smythe-sewn, $5.00
Michael Conway, *The Odyssey Singer*
    88 pp, smythe-sewn, $5.00
Eugene Lesser, *Drug Abuse in Marin County*
    136 pp, smythe-sewn, $8.95
Adele Langendorf, *Denial*
    64 pp, smythe-sewn, $5.00
William Witherup, *Collected Poems*
    224 pp, smythe-sewn, $10.00

Floating Island I
    120 pp, smythe-sewn, $6.95
Floating Island II
    184 pp, perfectbound, $8.95
Floating Island III
    160 pp, perfectbound, $12.95